BETTER RIDING
THROUGH EXERCISE

by

Linda Pearce
Dip FTST, FSMT

Illustrations by

Carole Vincer

KENILWORTH PRESS

First published in Great Britain by
The Kenilworth Press Limited,
Addington, Buckingham, MK18 2JR

© The Kenilworth Press Limited 1999
Reprinted 2003

British Library Cataloguing in Publication Data
A catalogue record for this book is available from the British Library.

ISBN 1-872119-11-5

Typeset by Kenilworth Press

Printed in Great Britain by Westway Offset

CONTENTS

Introduction

Many riders work hard at their riding, but their efforts do not always deliver the required results. Frustration and disappointment can set in, and riders find they reach a training plateau, unable to make progress or eradicate persistent faults. Sometimes this is due to a lack of experience or skill, but frequently it can be attributed to the rider's physical limitations. Irregularities in posture, muscle weakness, old injuries, poor aerobic fitness or lack of flexibility will not be overcome simply by spending more time in the saddle – indeed they are often magnified. The bottom line is that the horse's performance is hampered by his rider and his potential never realised.

Sadly, riding and mucking out are not enough to keep you fit. They merely keep you active. And whilst some riders consider themselves to be fit, the very act of riding can lead to adaptive shortening of muscles (as described on page 8) and with it a loss of flexibility. Nor is it necessarily the case that **all** types of exercises are beneficial to riders. Indeed, unless the exercises are riding-specific they may even be counter-productive.

Written by a sports therapist, fitness expert and rider, this book identifies common rider problems, and offers easy, lasting solutions through a programme of effective exercises and stretches. Specifically tailored for everyday riders as well as dressage, jumping, eventing and long-distance enthusiasts, the exercises are aimed at improving suppleness and strength, endurance and aerobic capacity, and eliminating crookedness and stiffness. They are designed to make the rider more effective and better balanced in the saddle, and, as a result, allow the horse to be more comfortable in his work and to develop athletically.

Once learned, the exercise programme outlined in this Picture Guide should take you only 20–30 minutes to complete, depending on the level of individual exercises you are capable of performing.

After all, riders are no different from other athletes (yes, riders **are** athletes) so recognising the need to work out should be seen as a positive step towards better riding. So get fit and stay fit, and enjoy your riding more and for longer. Your horse will thank you for it.

CAUTION

If you are diabetic, asthmatic, epileptic or have any other on-going medical complaint that may be adversely affected by following this exercise plan, please consult your doctor.

EQUIPMENT NEEDED

In addition to this book you will need:
• comfortable, loose or stretchy clothing • hand-held weights (or make do with cans of food, such as baked beans)/ankle weights 1–3kg (2–7lbs) • cross trainers or running shoes

Optional extras:
• heart-rate monitor • bicycle/rowing machine • walking boots • a friend to exercise with

Rider's reasons to exercise

To ride well we need: energy, flexibility, muscular balance, strength, muscular and cardiovascular endurance, and mental awareness. All these components will be required in varying degrees every time we ride. During competition both physical and mental requirements will have to adjust to the increased demand.

Following a sensible eating plan, combined with the exercises outlined in this book will increase your energy levels.

Balance and posture will improve with the development of strength and flexibility. Muscular and cardiovascular endurance will rapidly improve with the inclusion of some moderate aerobic activity such as walking, jogging, cycling or swimming.

Various studies have clearly shown that regular exercise provides additional benefits. These include: stronger ligaments and tendons, sharper reactions, higher levels of concentration, better memory, increased confidence, proprioception (body awareness). All of these are tremendously important to the rider who wishes to be more effective and

kinder to his trusty steed. Added to this, working out regularly can boost your immune system, increase your bone density, and help you shed unwanted body fat.

Even if you currently find riding easy and enjoyable you will find specific exercises identified just for you to help improve your effectiveness in the saddle.

In truth, every rider would benefit from being fitter and more supple, but to convince you, try answering these questions:
- Do you get out of breath going upstairs?
- Do you break into a sweat mucking out or grooming?
- Could your general riding position be improved?
- Does your instructor make the same corrections week in week out?
- Do you wish that riding were less of an effort?

If you answered 'yes' to any of the above questions you and your horse will benefit from you starting a fitness programme **right now!**

Common riding problems

The faults discussed here are extremely common and can even be seen in riders at the highest levels. To eliminate them the riding-specific training programme set out in this book should be followed in total. If you can rectify these problems, it is highly likely that other persistent riding problems will disappear too.

ABDOMINAL AND THIGH MUSCLES

Abdominal muscles facilitate forward movement from the waist and assist in maintenance of correct posture and balance.

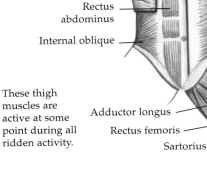

Rectus abdominus

Internal oblique

External oblique

These thigh muscles are active at some point during all ridden activity.

Adductor longus

Rectus femoris

Sartorius

Adaptive shortening (see page 8), weakness or injury to any muscles in the abdomen, hip and thigh will reduce rider efficiency.

HIP MUSCLES

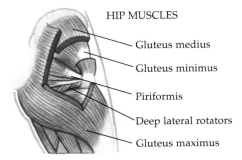

Gluteus medius

Gluteus minimus

Piriformis

Deep lateral rotators

Gluteus maximus

The muscles in the hip area have a variety of tasks to carry out whilst riding. Riders often suffer with over-tightening of the deep lateral rotators, sometimes causing sciatica. Gluteus maximus brings the body from a forward to an upright position.

THE CROOKED RIDER – Note especially the asymmetry of the shoulders, spine, waist and hips.

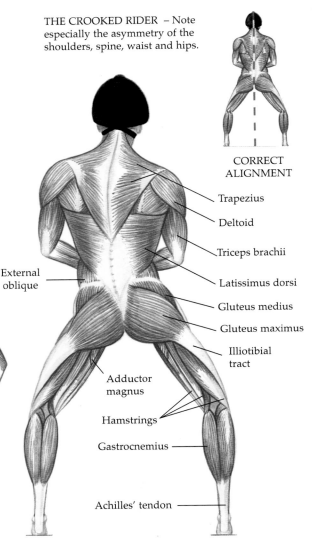

CORRECT ALIGNMENT

Trapezius

Deltoid

Triceps brachii

Latissimus dorsi

Gluteus medius

Gluteus maximus

Illiotibial tract

Adductor magnus

Hamstrings

Gastrocnemius

Achilles' tendon

Crookedness/collapsed hip

Whilst crookedness / collapsed hip may be obvious to our instructors and even ourselves, we are unable to maintain the necessary corrections whilst riding. From the illustration, we can see that the rider has shortening of the muscles to the right of the lumbar spine. The right hip is lifted and as a result further problems can be seen: the right shoulder is dropped, the head is tilted, the rider has to grip with the thigh, giving an insecure and ineffective lower leg. In an effort to make these corrections the rider usually attempts to work harder. Because the muscles have adaptively shortened (see page 8) they will work less efficiently. As a result they cannot sustain the activity, and the rider gives up, feeling tired and frustrated with his performance – and that of his horse.

Sadly, crooked riders make crooked horses. However, practice can make perfect, but you must have the correct tools for the job.

Weak abdominal muscles

The abdominal wall is a unique arrangement of muscles providing protection for internal organs. They are required in nearly all movements. Working together they allow you to bend forward from the waist. Internal and external obliques enable you to rotate from the waist and to bend the trunk to the side. The transversus abdominus will force expiration (breathing out) when pulled inward and helps to hold the abdominal area flat. These muscles provide stability for the trunk, allowing you to use your arms and legs for co-ordinated and independent movements.

Weak abdominals lead to poor balance, poor posture, inability to progress athletically, and the extremely common complaint amongst riders, chronic back pain.

It is important for you as a rider to develop as much abdominal strength as you can. The exercise plan in this book will help you achieve this.

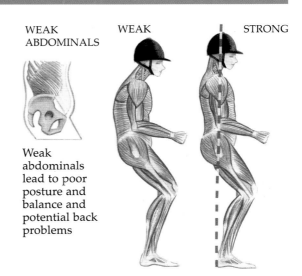

WEAK ABDOMINALS WEAK STRONG

Weak abdominals lead to poor posture and balance and potential back problems

Weak, unsupporting abdominals mean a poor riding position. Any corrections made whilst riding cannot be maintained without residual strength being present. This can only be achieved through muscle-specific strength training.

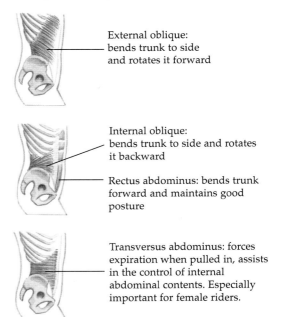

External oblique: bends trunk to side and rotates it forward

Internal oblique: bends trunk to side and rotates it backward

Rectus abdominus: bends trunk forward and maintains good posture

Transversus abdominus: forces expiration when pulled in, assists in the control of internal abdominal contents. Especially important for female riders.

Flexibility programme

Flexibility, or lack of it, determines exactly how much movement we have around a joint. This is referred to as Range of Movement (ROM). We can measure ROM by observing the muscles in their: outer range (fully stretched); inner range (fully shortened); and mid-range (between the two extremes).

Whilst riding, your muscle action will mostly be somewhere around the mid-range, but some ridden activities require riders to use their muscles at the inner (shortened) range for much of the time. As a result, it is quite common for a rider to have shortened hip flexors. If these muscles have become **adaptively shortened** (through habitual use in the inner range) they may then pull on the lumbar spine, resulting in back pain. Adaptive shortening of the quadriceps, hamstrings and back muscles themselves can all lead to back pain and reduce muscle efficiency. If your muscles do not respond to their maximum potential and in isolation, when, for example, you try to apply a leg aid, you could give confusing signals to your horse. So it is important to be able to take all the muscles of the body

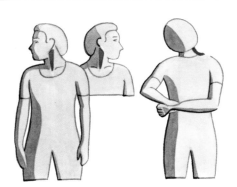

Neck (upper trapezius and sternocleidomastoid muscles)
All disciplines will benefit.
• Sitting or standing, turn head to take chin level with right shoulder.
• Keep shoulders in line with the hips and support the spine by tightening the abdominal muscles.
• Return head to face forward before repeating to the left. Hold for 6–20 seconds each side.
• Take your right hand around to the back and clasp your wrist. Maintain this position at waist height while tilting your head to the same side. Return to start position and repeat to the left side. Hold for 6–20 seconds.

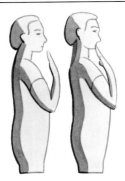

Posterior neck muscles
All disciplines – particularly useful for riders with a tendency to look down or protract the head forward while riding, upsetting the balance of both horse and rider.
• Sit or stand, and support the spine by tightening the abdominal muscles.
• Look straight ahead, tuck your chin in – place a hand on your chin and push gently against it.
Tightness in these neck muscles can lead to headaches.

through their full range of movement of both contraction and extension.

Other factors affecting flexibility for riding are build, muscle imbalance, age, old or recent injury.

It is recommended that these stretches be performed daily to **warm** muscles, so include a 5-minute warm-up before you start – a brisk walk will suffice. While stretching, keep breathing evenly; do not hold your breath. Feel each stretch and enjoy the sensation – it should **not** cause you pain. You can hold the stretches for longer than stipulated if you have just taken part in strenuous exercise or have been riding.

Once you are familiar with the exercises you will find they take you just a few minutes, but the benefits to you as a rider can be extremely significant. You will probably notice a difference in your horse's way of going. Be patient. Improvements will be gradual, and once achieved will need to be maintained. Missing odd days will not significantly reduce the effect. However, stopping for a week or longer will greatly reduce your ability.

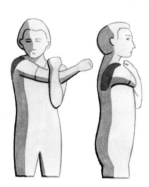

Shoulder (deltoid muscles)
All disciplines will benefit.
• Sitting or standing, reach right arm diagonally across body; keep arm at shoulder height.
• With left hand hug the right arm closer to chest. To change emphasis take right arm underneath the armpit. Repeat to left shoulder. Hold for 6–20 seconds on each side.
This stretch should not be performed if you have injured this joint area. Ensure there is no twisting at the waist.

Back of upper arm (triceps muscles)
All disciplines will benefit.
• Sitting or standing, take right arm upwards, drop the hand down behind the head and between shoulder blades. Elbow should be pointing to the ceiling.
• Take left arm around behind the head and clasp the elbow, easing it inward and backward. Keep the right arm close to your head. Keep chin off the chest. Repeat with left arm. Hold for 6–20 seconds on each side.

Flexibility programme cont.

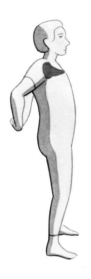

← Chest and front of shoulders (pectorals, anterior deltoids)

All disciplines – improves posture, balance and breathing.
- Standing, clasp hands behind your back; pull backwards, opening the front of the chest and shoulders. Keep looking forward with chin off chest. Hold for 6–20 seconds.
- Altering the height of your clasped hands will change the emphasis.
- To alter the emphasis still further use a towel held at varying widths and heights.

Do not attempt this exercise if you have a history of shoulder dislocation.

**Upper back and shoulders (rhomboids, →
trapezius, posterior deltoids)**

All disciplines, especially riders who want to improve upper body position and balance.
- Stand with feet hip-distance apart and knees slightly bent.
- Extend arms, clasp hands together and ease shoulder blades apart.
- Keep abdominal muscles tight and chin off chest. Hold for 6–20 seconds.

To vary this exercise and to include a stretch to the latissimus dorsi (back) muscles, clasp both hands around a strong post (a fence post would do) and lean backward.

Forearms (flexors and extensors)

All disciplines, especially riders whose horses take a strong contact.
- Sit or stand, place palms together as shown.
- Keeping hands in contact with each other and with fingers extended ease the heel of the hands towards the floor. Hold for 6–20 seconds.
- Take right arm straight out to the front at shoulder height.
- With the left hand placed across the knuckles of the right hand ease the right palm towards your body. Hold for 6–20 seconds. Repeat to the left arm.

These exercises can reveal limitations if you have suffered an injury to the wrist that has resulted in swelling. Use caution whilst trying to improve flexibility.

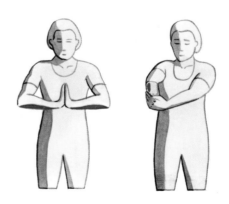

Calf muscles (gastrocnemius and soleus)

All disciplines will benefit.

• Stage 1 – Place hands on a wall, take right leg back and place foot flat on the floor.

• Right foot should point straight forward in line with knee and hip. Keeping heel in contact with the floor, lean body weight towards wall.

• Stage 2 – Lift right heel and bring foot half a step closer to left foot; place flat on floor. Use the wall for balance and bend the right knee until stretch is felt. Hold each position for 6–20 seconds. Repeat to left leg.

Turning toes in or out in each position will alter the emphasis to the inner or outer portions of the muscles involved.

Front of thighs (quadriceps)

All disciplines, especially show jumping, cross-country and hunting.

• Lie on your front with forehead on left forearm.

• Grasp right foot with right hand, keep knees together and hold foot into buttock. To further extend this stretch press hip into floor. Hold for 6–20 seconds. Repeat to left thigh. Can be done standing if at a competition.

If unable to reach the foot in this way your quadriceps have adaptively shortened. Loop a towel around the ankle to make up the shortfall. Correct and repeated exercises over several weeks will help the muscles to lengthen again.

Inner thighs (hip adductors)

All disciplines, especially dressage.

• Sit upright, legs straight in front.

• Make fists and place on the floor behind hips.

• Move legs to astride position. Pushing down through your fists, lean body slightly forward from the hip, spine straight. Hold for 6–20 seconds. Easing slightly further forward whilst easing legs apart further will develop greater flexibility.

Pelvis should tilt forward whilst moving pubic bone back to effect a stretch. Do not allow the spine to bend as this will stretch spinal tissue. Do not allow knees to bend as stress may be placed on the medial ligament of the knee.

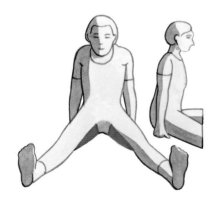

Flexibility programme cont.

Back of thigh and buttocks (hamstring and gluteus maximus)

All disciplines, especially eventing and endurance.
• Lie on your back, knees bent, feet flat on the floor.
• Lift one knee, clasp your hands behind the knee and hug towards the chest. Straighten the other leg. Hold for 6–20 seconds. From this position gradually straighten the raised leg. Use only the quadriceps (front of leg) to straighten it. Hold for 6–20 seconds. Repeat with other leg.
If you have difficulty reaching, place a towel around the back of the thigh, just below the knee. Keep hips in contact with the floor. Pulling your toes towards you encourages a stretch in the gastrocnemius muscle (calf). To further increase flexibility, alter the emphasis on the inner or outer hamstring by rotating the leg – inward and outward.

Buttock and piriformis muscle

All disciplines will benefit.
• Lie on your back, knees bent, feet flat on the floor.
• Cross right ankle over left knee, clasp hands together behind the thigh of the left leg and ease towards you. Tightly pull in your abdominal muscles to prevent any arching of the back. Hold for 6–20 seconds. Repeat to the other leg.
This exercise stretches the piriformis muscle which is located deep in the pelvis area. Tightness in this muscle can sometimes place stress on the sciatic nerve causing pain in the lower back.

Spine, waist and buttocks (obliques and hip abductors)

All disciplines will benefit.
• Lie flat on your back, left arm outstretched Bend your left knee.
• Place right hand on the left knee and ease left knee over right leg until a stretch is felt in the areas indicated. Ensure that both shoulders stay in contact with the floor. Only go as far as is comfortable. Hold for 6–20 seconds. Repeat to other side. May be held for longer if this is a problem area.
Due to the stretch in the spine you may hear or feel some clicks. This is perfectly normal.

Lumbar spine and spinal extensors

All disciplines will benefit.

• Stage 1 – Lying flat on an exercise mat or folded blanket bring your knees towards your chest.

• Hold arms behind the knees.

• Hug the knees into the chest and towards your shoulders until your coccyx (tail bone) lifts off the floor. Hold for 6–20 seconds.

If you feel stiff in the lower back/waist area or have suffered a lower-back problem in the past it would benefit you to vary the position of your knees from central to slightly left and right. Always return to a neutral position before changing emphasis.

• Stage 2 – Turn over and support upper body on forearms. Keep forearms in contact with the mat and push hips into the floor. Hold for 6–20 seconds.

Do not straighten arms or push up in this position as it could cause damage to spinal tissues and joints. This exercise will also stretch abdominals.

STAGE 1

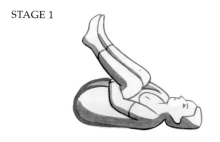

STAGE 2

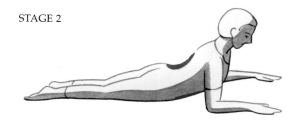

Hip flexors

All disciplines will benefit.

• Begin by lungeing forward with the left leg.

• Allow heel of right foot to lift off the floor, if necessary. Place hands on hips or a chair for balance; push right hip forward (without twisting at the waist) keep abdominals firm and the torso upright.

• Provided you do not have knee problems progress to kneeling position and slowly perform movements shown in dotted lines to fully extended position. Allow 60 seconds per leg to perform thoroughly and release stretch by reversing movements.

Tightening the abdominals will prevent unwanted pelvic movement. Pelvic movement may cause the spine to hyper-extend, which could be harmful.

Strength training programme

Muscular strength and endurance is essential to the rider and his horse. A strong, balanced rider is easier to carry and understand (through being able to give clearer signals). Age is not a limiting factor. Indeed, beyond your late twenties your muscle mass will begin to diminish at the approximate rate of 3kg (7lbs) a decade, making it even more important for the adult rider to develop and maintain a strong, **balanced** body.

You should include specific strength exercises, some involving weights, in your weekly routine. They will not only increase your strength but also, if performed at the correct speed and with a correct and safe technique will produce some terrific side-effects:

- a decrease in overall body fat
- improved posture and balance
- improved endurance and tone

Female riders need not worry that the exercises will cause them to develop unsightly bulging muscles. Instead they are more likely to trim down and tone up, enhancing body shape.

Please use the guidelines opposite for all strength exercises.

Strength Training Guidelines

Effort level

1–2	Requires no effort
3	I can just feel the weight
4	Feels heavy but okay
5	Feels difficult – getting uncomfortable
6	It's difficult – can't speak
7	Difficult to keep weight moving
8	Not able to move weight
9	Not able to move weight but can maintain grip
10	Have to put weight down before I drop it

Effort level	Sessions/week	
4	2–3	Absolute beginner
5–6	2–3	Regular exercise
7–9	2–3	Already uses weights
9–10	1–2	Advanced trainer

- Do a 5-minute warm-up before starting.
- Each exercise should be completed only once.
- The movements should be slow and controlled (faster is not effective and could cause injury), taking 6 seconds to lift and 4 seconds to lower. This applies even when a limb is used as the only resistance.
- Joints must not lock between repetitions.
- The muscles should be loaded by weight for at least 60 seconds (6 repetitions). Keep moving throughout the exercise. If you can do more than 12 repetitions (120 seconds) then you need to increase the weight.
- Breathing – a simple rule is: exertion = exhale – you will inhale automatically!

Upper back and shoulders (trapezius, rhomboids and posterior deltoids)

All disciplines – important for posture and balance.
- Sit upright with abdominals tight and feet flat on the floor.
- Incline forward from the hips, make a fist, and with arms slightly bent at elbows, lift elbows high, squeezing shoulder blades together.
When keeping abdominals tight remember to exhale while lifting. Do 8–12 repetitions with 1–3kg (2–7lbs) hand-held weights. Do without weights the first time. If this is difficult do not add weights until it is easy.

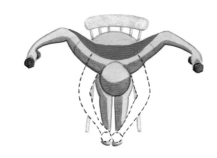

Front top of arm (biceps)

All disciplines – combined with triceps exercise helps prevent the onset of a condition known as tennis elbow, which is a common condition amongst riders.

- Seated on both seat bones, sit tall.
- Tighten abdominals to maintain back support.
- Open chest by drawing shoulders back and rotating arm 30 degrees.
- Keeping top of arm close to ribcage begin lift – lift only until arm cannot bend any further. Elbows should remain aiming towards the floor.

To vary the emphasis rotate the hand weight to an upright position and do 8–12 repetitions.

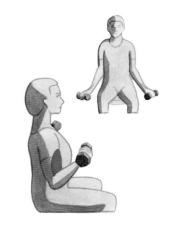

Shoulders (deltoids)

All disciplines – correctional exercise for riders with poor upper body strength and posture.

- Begin seated or standing. Tighten abdominals to maintain back support.
- Lift slowly to shoulder height only.
- Use hand-held weights if you can complete more than 12 repetitions.
- Remember to keep looking straight ahead. If standing, keep knees soft (slightly bent).

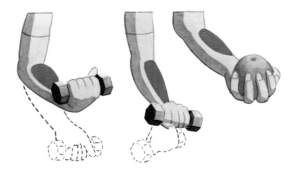

Wrist and finger exercises

All disciplines will benefit. These exercises are not designed to give a grip of iron, but to ensure even muscular development throughout the arm, reducing the risk of injury and improving body awareness.

- Keep forearm supported on a table or your knee, with palm uppermost. Make a fist or hold small weights and flex toward elbow. Do 8–12 repetitions.
- Turn forearm to face palm towards the floor. With a fist or small hand weight lift toward elbow. Do 8–12 repetitions.
- Lastly, holding an apple or tennis ball in each hand squeeze and release 8–12 times.

Strength training programme cont.

Back (latissimus dorsi)
All disciplines will benefit.
• Holding a hand weight – begin with 3kg (7lbs) and build to 5kg (12lbs) – lie fully supported on a bench or table.
• Begin with weight held with slightly bent arms in line with the chest. Lower as far as comfortable. Repeat 8–12 times.
As you become stronger throughout your body, decrease the support by lying across a bench or stool. Remember to use your abdominal muscles. Exercise caution if you have ever suffered a shoulder injury.

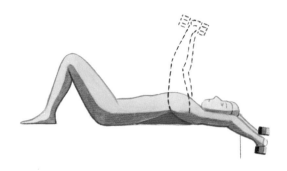

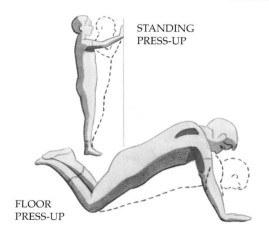

STANDING PRESS-UP

FLOOR PRESS-UP

Upper mid-back, chest and back of arms (rhomboids, pectorals, triceps)
All disciplines will benefit.
• Begin with standing press-ups: stand arm's length from wall, keeping body in alignment. Lean forward to touch forehead to wall, push back to upright position. Repeat 8–12 times.
Altering height and width of arms will alter emphasis and increase all round strength of muscles worked.
• Progress to floor press-ups: maintain body alignment – weight should rest on hands and thigh (**not** on knee cap). If the body sags you are not strong enough. Try again in three weeks.
• Progress to full press-ups with legs extended if you can.
Altering width of arms will alter emphasis.

Abdominals
All disciplines will benefit.
• Lie on an exercise mat or folded blanket to protect spine. Keep knees bent, feet close to buttocks.
• Level 1 – Place hands on thighs, pull abdominals inward and reach toward knees, lifting shoulder blades off the floor. Exhale as you sit up. Aim to do 20 repetitions.
• Level 2 – Fold arms across chest. Pull abdominals inward and lift shoulder blades off the floor. When comfortable doing 20 repetitions, progress to:
• Level 3 – Take knuckles to ears keeping the elbows out. Hold abdominals in and lift shoulder blades off floor.
• To place emphasis on the obliques, keep right knuckle to ear, lift and reach left hand to the outside of right knee. Repeat 12 times and change sides.
If neck muscles tire, rest and then continue.

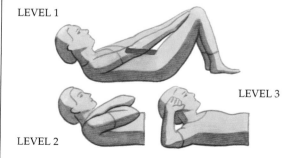

LEVEL 1

LEVEL 2

LEVEL 3

Lower leg (gastrocnemius and soleus)

All disciplines will benefit.

• With a chair or wall for support, stand on a step or bricks.

• Rise onto toes and slowly lower, making sure the heel drops lower than the toes. Repeat 8–12 times.

• Progress to standing on one leg at a time. Repeat 8–12 times with each leg.

• A hand weight can be held to increase resistance for further progression.

• The seated version should also be included as it changes the emphasis. Hand weights should rest on the thigh.

Remember to keep your spine straight and use the abdominals for support.

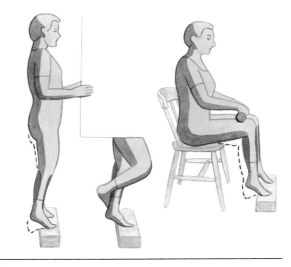

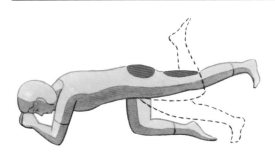

Back of thigh and buttock (gluteus maximus and hamstrings)

All disciplines will benefit.

• Begin in kneeling position.

• Support body on forearms and straighten left leg.

• Raise to hip height and lift and lower. (Leg can be bent while lifting and lowering if too difficult.) The toes should just touch the floor on lowering. Do 8–12 repetitions.

• Keep leg extended at hip height and bend and straighten it a further 8–12 times before repeating on other side.

Be careful not to sag in the middle and maintain position. Use abdominals for support.

Lower and mid-back

All disciplines will benefit.

• Level 1 – Lie face down, arms by your sides, palms up. Forehead should touch the mat. Keep looking at the floor and maintain head and neck alignment. Raise upwards. Hips, legs and feet should remain in contact with the floor. Repeat 8–12 times. Once easy, progress to:

• Level 2 – Same position as above except knuckles come to temples and arms are also lifted. Repeat 8–12 times.

• Level 3 (advanced) – As Level 2 but arms reach out level with ears while lifting. To increase resistance further you can pull arms back as you raise, and reach out again as you lower.

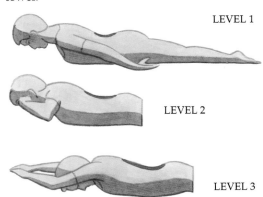

LEVEL 1

LEVEL 2

LEVEL 3

Strength training programme cont.

Back of thighs (hamstrings)
All disciplines will benefit.
• Place chair or stool against a wall for security.
• Lie on exercise mat and place hands, palms down, under hips. Rest both feet on the chair with knees in line with hips.
• Slowly raise and lower the pelvis while pushing down with your heels. Repeat 8–12 times.
• Progression –Take right leg over left and work only the left hamstrings. Do 8–12 repetitions with each leg.

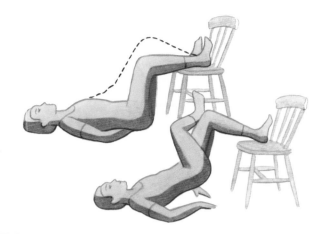

Front of thighs (quadriceps)
All disciplines will benefit.
• Level 1 – Lie completely flat. Pull toes toward you. Lock right leg straight. Raise right leg 6 ins (15cm) from the floor, then lower it almost to the floor. Repeat 8–12 times. Repeat to left leg.
• Level 2 – Recline on elbows as illustrated and repeat as above.
Increase muscle endurance and learn your dressage test by signing letters with your foot. Remember: only 6 ins (15cm) from the floor. This is a hard one, but don't give up.
• Level 3 – Sit almost upright, place palms just behind your hips for support and repeat as above.

Front of thighs (quadriceps)
All disciplines will benefit.
• Hold a towel over your shoulders and lean against a smooth surface, e.g. double-glazed door, full-length mirror.
• Keeping shoulders back and hips in contact with surface, slowly lower until hips are level with knees. Try not to let heels come off the floor nor let the knees bend in front of the vertical.
• Push up until legs are almost straight.
• Repeat whole movement 8–12 times.
This exercise is also popular with those who ski, as it significantly strengthens the thighs.

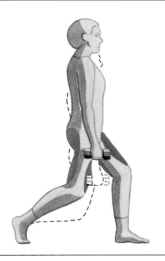

Thighs and buttocks (quadriceps, hamstrings and gluteus muscles)

All disciplines will benefit.
- Take a step forward with left foot.
- Maintaining body alignment, i.e. ear, shoulder, hip, raise right heel and bend knee.
- Maintain vertical position of left lower leg.
- Dip down allowing the right knee to come into alignment.
- Raise and repeat 8–12 times with each leg.

Use gluteal muscles and abdominals to maintain pelvic stability. Do not allow leading leg to bend over the toes – this will place stress on the ligaments of the knee. To increase resistance hold hand weights from 2kg (4lbs) upwards.

Inner thighs (adductors)

All disciplines will benefit.
- Lie as illustrated, or straighten upper leg and place on a chair (if you choose this option you will need to lie fully on your side).
- Straighten right leg, pull toes towards you.
- Rotate the leg so that the heel lifts off the floor.
- Lift to chair height only (either option).
- Slowly lower, lightly touch the floor with outside of foot.
- Repeat 8–12 times, turn over and repeat with other leg.

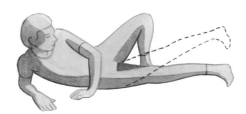

Outer thighs and hips (abductors)

All disciplines will benefit.
- Lie on your right side, head supported on hand.
- Bend right leg behind you and place left hand on the floor. Keep hips in line with shoulders.
- Allow left hip and leg to rotate slightly forwards so that heel is off the floor.
- Maintain position, lift and lower, lightly touch toe to floor between repetitions.
- Repeat 8–12 times with each leg. Use ankle weights for increased resistance.

Leg need only be lifted 18–24 ins (45–60cm) off the floor.

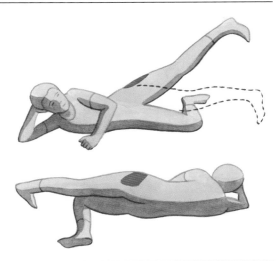

Strength training programme cont.

Back of upper arm (triceps)

All disciplines will benefit.

• Place hands behind you on a chair, bench or step. Take your body weight onto your arms and walk feet away from you (legs fully extended will make you work harder).

• Dip downward until shoulder and elbow are level (you can dip lower as you become stronger). Return to start position and repeat 8–12 times.

Abdominals should remain firm. Avoid this exercise if you have a recent shoulder or wrist injury or a history of shoulder dislocation.

Back of upper arm (triceps)

All disciplines will benefit.

• Lie supported on a bench or exercise mat on the floor.

• Hold a small hand weight (1kg / 2lbs) in your right hand. Place across chest just above left shoulder.

• To maintain elbow high position, place left hand just below elbow.

• Fully straighten arm and return to start position.

• Repeat 8–12 times and then repeat to left arm.

• Variation – Both triceps can be worked simultaneously by taking elbows high and lowering weights to shoulders the same side. This is more advanced as there is no support.

A useful addition or alternative to the triceps exercise above.

Aerobic conditioning

All riders will benefit from aerobic conditioning, but particularly event riders, endurance riders, new riders and overweight riders. Aerobic exercise increases the efficiency of your heart and lungs. It involves working the body in the presence of oxygen, as opposed to anaerobically (without oxygen) as in strength training exercises.

All muscle activity (including riding) requires energy. The carbohydrate you eat largely provides that energy, and the body stores it in your muscles in the form of glycogen. Glycogen (muscle energy) is released by the oxygen carried in your blood supply. So having a strong heart and efficient lungs will make muscle action (power and strength) more readily available to you.

The simplest form of aerobic exercise is walking. It involves little risk of injury and the only equipment needed is a decent pair of shoes/boots – and perhaps a dog! It can be done at any time of the day. Other aerobic activities include running, swimming, cycling, rowing and dancing.

If you are healthy (if you have any concerns, consult your doctor) your aerobic training-zone pulse rate will be between 60% and 90% of maximum heart rate (MHR). Using the simple formula of '220 minus your age' gives you a figure for your MHR, e.g.

220 – 35 years = MHR 185

You can then multiply that figure by 60% to give you a training-zone pulse rate in beats per minute (BPM):

185 x 60% = 111 BPM

Translated this means that you should expect your heart to be beating at the rate of 111 BPM during exercise.

The most reliable way to take your pulse is with a heart-rate monitor, but you can take it manually. Place two fingers on the carotid artery located near your windpipe. Take your pulse for 15 seconds then multiply it by 4 = BPM. Continue exercising while taking your pulse; stopping will make it drop. If your pulse rate is higher than required, reduce effort; if too low, increase effort. Your pulse rate should be monitored regularly throughout your work-outs, ensuring continuous, effective and safe training.

If you are very unfit or overweight, begin your training programme at 50% of MHR.

Recommended training frequency: 3–5 days per week.

Intensity: 60–90% MHR (endurance and event riders should aim for training intensities between 85–90% of MHR).

Duration: 20–60 minutes, plus 5-minute warm-up beforehand and 5-minute warm-down afterwards.

Healthy eating

If you want your body to work to its maximum potential you need to look at the fuel you put in. Sports nutritionists recommend that we cut down on fat for health reasons, not just when losing weight, by using skimmed/semi-skimmed milk, low-fat dairy products or vegetable-based alternatives. Further health benefits can be gained by reducing tea and coffee intake to a maximum of four cups per day. Both beverages have a diuretic and dehydrating effect. Sugary drinks or snacks should be avoided if possible. Too much sugar in your diet can lead to tiredness and even depression. Salt can also cause dehydration, which no athlete would want.

Fruit and vegetables should be eaten daily with a minimum of three portions of each. When planning healthy meals an excellent basis would be jacket potatoes, wholemeal pasta, brown rice or wholemeal/granary bread. Many dieticians recommend that we cut down on the number of eggs we eat; and also on the amount of red meat we consume – chicken, turkey or white fish are good lower fat alternatives. They also suggest that we replace some traditional meals with all vegetable meals.

Always fuel up for your busy day with a good carbohydrate breakfast: cereals and toast is a good start. If breakfast is skipped you are likely to crave a sweet or savoury snack. In case of a refuelling emergency, keep some cereal bars or fruit handy.

Last but not least, try to increase your water intake – very few people consume enough. Experts suggests that we should drink 2 litres – approx. 4.5 pints – per day. Drinking water with other beverages and meals will quickly build your intake. Water is especially important before, during, and after exercise.

To reduce body fat or to ensure you don't accumulate more than you would like, try to cut down on your daily intake and take more exercise. For a 200kcal per day reduction reduce 100kcal of food, e.g. 2 biscuits, and take a 20-minute brisk walk to use 100kcal of energy. Eating just 50 calories per day more than you use would equal a yearly surplus of 18,000 calories or 3kg (7lbs) of fat.

In short, too much of any foodstuff will be deposited as fat. Intake must equal output or be less than output in order to lose weight, but remember to allow time for any exercises or eating changes to take effect.

50 calories of food	50 calories of exercise
1 brandy	10 mins brisk walk
1 pat of butter	5 mins jog
1 digestive biscuit	10 mins strength training
1 tbsp of cream	10 mins moderate cycling

And if you are tempted to indulge in 'forbidden' foods, remember: 'all things in moderation' and you won't go far wrong.

Body type/age

Riders, like the rest of us, come in all shapes and sizes. These differences can be partly explained by our **body type**. We can recognise three main body types: endomorphs, mesomorphs, and ectomorphs.

If you have a rounder figure and tend to put on and store fat you are an **endomorph.**

If you have good bone structure, with a muscular figure, you are a **mesomorph** – even in women the chest will be broad with the shoulders wider than the waist.

Ectomorphs tend to be tall with fine, long limbs and little body fat; they are not overly muscled.

In reality, the majority of us are a mixture of these three but with a tendency towards one type.

When exercising, it is important to ensure that we do not attempt to achieve the impossible. If we are truly an ectomorph we will have great difficulty in transforming ourselves into a meso- or endomorph! If in doubt about your fitness goals contact a personal trainer or fitness expert.

We have already stated that **age** is not a limiting factor when it comes to exercise. However, it would be prudent for the mature rider to start a new exercise programme at the easiest level.

Changes to body shape and rider effectiveness through exercise can be made at any age, but as we grow older we can expect these changes to happen more gradually. Older riders therefore need to be more patient about seeing the results of their efforts. Also, older riders may have to work longer to overcome a physical limitation, purely because it has established itself over a longer period of time.

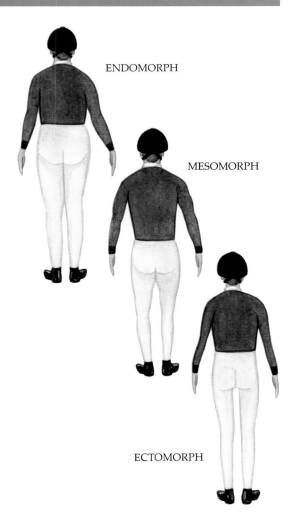

ENDOMORPH

MESOMORPH

ECTOMORPH

Women especially, from teens to senior citizens, should regularly take part in weight-bearing exercise. Walking is ideal, and regular strength training, in addition to providing muscular strength, has been shown to increase bone density throughout the body. Since riders are at greater risk than most of having broken bones (through falls), increasing bone density through exercise will help to lessen the chance of injury.

Exercises to avoid

All of the exercises illustrated on this page should be avoided by the average rider. They cannot be recommended because they include movements that could potentially be damaging to various tissues and facet joints of the spine.

Whilst the mounted exercises shown are aimed at improving rider flexibility, it can be more effectively achieved, without risk of injury, through the exercises on pages 8–13.

Safer alternatives to the unmounted abdominal and hamstring exercises shown below can be found on pages 16 and 12 respectively.

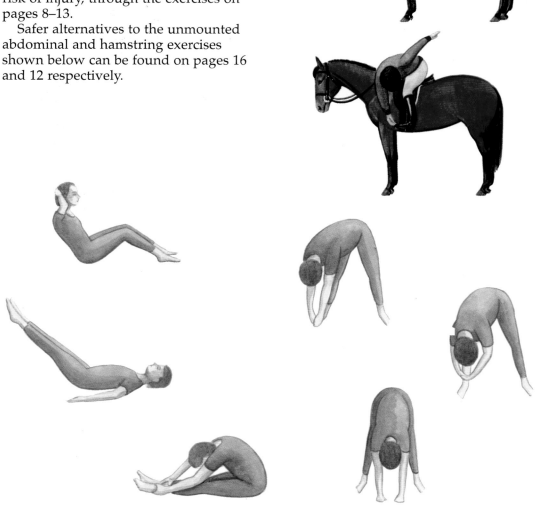